PREHISTORIC EXPLORER

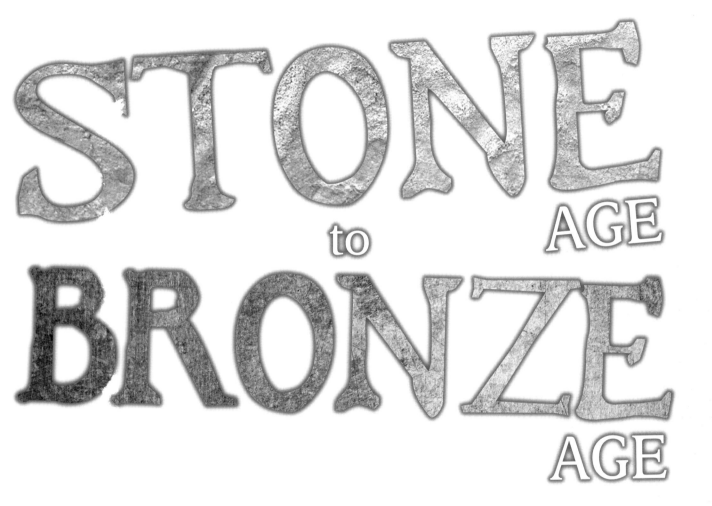

STONE AGE to BRONZE AGE

by
Grace Jones

BookLife PUBLISHING

BookLife Publishing Ltd,
King's Lynn, Norfolk
PE30 4LS, UK

ISBN: 978-1-80155-677-4

A catalogue record for this book
is available from the British Library.

Written by:
Grace Jones

Edited by:
Charlie Ogden

Designed by:
Drue Rintoul

Photo Credits
Abbreviations: l—left, r—right, b—bottom, t—top, c—centre, m—middle.

4bl – By Portable Antiquities Scheme [CC BY–SA 3.0 (http://creativecommons.org/licenses/by–sa/3.0)], via Wikimedia Commons. 4tr – By Prof saxx (Own work) [GFDL (http://www.gnu.org/copyleft/fdl.html) or CC–BY–SA–3.0 (http://creativecommons.org/licenses/by–sa/3.0/)], via Wikimedia Commons. 5 – AuntSpray. 6 – By Gunnar Creutz (Own work) [CC BY–SA 3.0 (http://creativecommons.org/licenses/by–sa/3.0)], via Wikimedia Commons. 7 – Wisbech Museum (www.wisbechmuseum.org.uk). 8l – Jule_Berlin. 8br – Chokniti Khongchum. 8br – Potapov Alexander. 9 – By Jack Versloot (originally posted to Flickr as Lascaux II) [CC BY 2.0 (http://creativecommons.org/licenses/by/2.0)], via Wikimedia Commons. 10tr, 10br – Wisbech Museum (www.wisbechmuseum. org.uk). 10bl – Ashley Dace [CC BY–SA 2.0 (http://creativecommons.org/licenses/by–sa/2.0)], via Wikimedia Commons. 11t – By Theroadislong (Own work) [CC BY–SA 3.0 (http://creativecommons.org/licenses/by–sa/3.0)], via Wikimedia Commons. 11b – Hanay [CC BY–SA 3.0 (http://creativecommons.org/licenses/by–sa/3.0)], via Wikimedia Commons. 12l – johnbraid. 13tr – Jule_Berlin. 13bl – Jule_Berlin. 14b – picturepartners. 15t – By Bluefinland at Finnish WikipediaPatrik Franzen (Own workKierikkikeskus) [Public domain], via Wikimedia Commons. 15b – By Wolfgang Sauber (Own work) [CC BY–SA 4.0 (http://creativecommons.org/licenses/by–sa/4.0)], via Wikimedia Commons. 16t – By Jim Champion (Own work) [GFDL (http://www.gnu.org/copyleft/fdl.html), CC–BY–SA–3.0 (http://creativecommons.org/licenses/by–sa/3.0/) or CC BY–SA 2.5–2.0–1.0 (http://creativecommons.org/licenses/by–sa/2.5–2.0–1.0)], via Wikimedia Commons 16b – Wisbech Museum (www.wisbechmuseum.org.uk). 17r – Fotos593. 17b – Anneka. 18t – Alan Simkins [CC BY–SA 2.0 (http://creativecommons.org/licenses/by–sa/2.0)], via Wikimedia Commons. 18b – Wisbech Museum (www.wisbechmuseum.org.uk). 19 – Wisbech Museum (www.wisbechmuseum.org.uk). 20t – Wisbech Museum (www.wisbechmuseum.org.uk). 20b – By Richard Avery (Own work) [CC BY–SA 4.0 (http://creativecommons.org/licenses/by–sa/4.0)], via Wikimedia Commons. 21t – By mari from tokyo, japan (bronze age boat) [CC BY 2.0 (http://creativecommons.org/licenses/by/2.0)], via Wikimedia Commons. 21b – By Gerdrey (Own work) [Public domain], via Wikimedia Commons. 22t – By USGS (World Wind (go)) [Public domain], via Wikimedia Commons. 22b – Helen Hotson. 23 – Wisbech Museum (www.wisbechmuseum.org.uk). 24t – Dudarev Mikhail. 24b – By Viv Hamilton at English Wikipedia [Public domain], via Wikimedia Commons. 25 – Wisbech Museum (www.wisbechmuseum.org.uk). 26t – Vicky Jirayu. 26b – Kiev. Victor. 27t – Henri et George. 27b – 1000 Words. 28tl – Fotocrisis. 28tr – By Immanuel Giel (Own work) [Public domain], via Wikimedia Commons. 28bl – dtopal. 28mbl – Simon Bratt. 29bl – dade72. 29bm – Radek Sturgolewski. 29br – Stefano Pellicciari. Images are courtesy of Shutterstock.com, unless stated otherwise. With thanks to Getty Images, Thinkstock Photo and iStockphoto.

CONTENTS

Words that look like **this** can be found in the glossary on page 31.

PREHISTORIC BRITAIN

*THE FIRST HUMANS ARRIVED IN BRITAIN AROUND 840,000 YEARS AGO, DURING A TIME KNOW AS THE **PREHISTORIC** PERIOD.*

We know this because there have been many discoveries that show signs of human life in this period. Human skeletons and many **artefacts** made out of **flint**, stone and bone have been unearthed by **archaeologists** all over Britain.

The Lascaux Caves in south-west France house some of the oldest cave paintings in the world, which date back to around 16,000 **BC**. Cave drawings are one of the earliest signs of human life to appear in the many prehistoric **cave-dwellings** found throughout Europe.

This hand axe, which was found on a beach in Happisburgh, England, would have been used to chop things such as tree branches.

The Happisburgh Haul

Archaeologists **excavating** a number of prehistoric sites in Happisburgh, on the eastern coast of England, uncovered around 80 tools made from stone and flint. **Historians** believe that the flint tools probably would have been used to cut objects and slice food. In 2013, a human footprint was uncovered in the ancient **estuary** mudflats at the site. This is the earliest sign of human life ever to be found in Britain and it is around 840,000 years old.

Long extinct species of animal, such as woolly mammoths and sabre-toothed cats, walked the Earth during the Early Stone Age. We know this because their fossilised remains and bones have been found all over the world and they have appeared in cave paintings from that time period.

THE BOXGROVE MAN

The Boxgrove Man is a 500,000 year old human fossil discovered by an archaeologist in West Sussex, England in 1993. We can work out roughly how old he is using the items and animals that he was buried with.

Found alongside his remains were many flint and stone tools as well as the animal remains of now extinct species of rhinoceros, bear and vole. The animals had been butchered, which suggests that they had been hunted or **scavenged**.

Who Were the First Settlers in Britain?

Although there is evidence of human life in Britain some 840,000 years ago, the first people to settle in Britain did so much later, in around 12,000 BC. At this time, Britain was extremely cold and **hunter-gatherers** survived by hunting animals, scavenging, fishing and gathering wild nuts and berries. They used tools made from natural materials that included stone, bone and wood.

THE STONE AGE

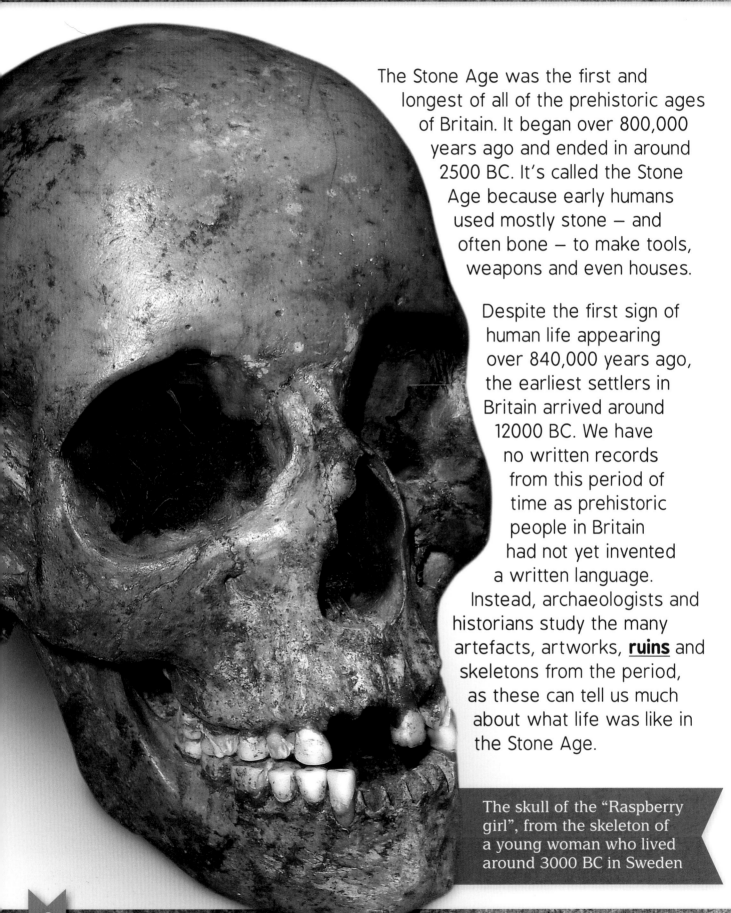

The Stone Age was the first and longest of all of the prehistoric ages of Britain. It began over 800,000 years ago and ended in around 2500 BC. It's called the Stone Age because early humans used mostly stone – and often bone – to make tools, weapons and even houses.

Despite the first sign of human life appearing over 840,000 years ago, the earliest settlers in Britain arrived around 12000 BC. We have no written records from this period of time as prehistoric people in Britain had not yet invented a written language. Instead, archaeologists and historians study the many artefacts, artworks, **ruins** and skeletons from the period, as these can tell us much about what life was like in the Stone Age.

The skull of the "Raspberry girl", from the skeleton of a young woman who lived around 3000 BC in Sweden

THE STONE AGE IS USUALLY DIVIDED INTO THREE PERIODS OF TIME. They are the Old Stone Age, the Middle Stone Age and the New Stone Age.

Old Stone Age
800,000–9600 BC

The Old Stone Age, also known as the Paleolithic Age, was the first and longest period of prehistoric history, starting around 800,000 years ago and ending around 9600 BC. Britain at this time was mostly covered in ice and went through several very long and extremely cold environmental periods called ice ages. Towards the end of the Old Stone Age, people began to settle in one place. These settlers were hunter-gatherers who used **primitive** stone tools and had previously found shelter in cave-dwellings.

MIDDLE STONE AGE
9600 BC–4000 BC

The Middle Stone Age – also known as the Mesolithic Age – began after the last ice age ended. This is when the warmer climate encouraged people to settle in more northerly territories, such as Scotland, and new plant and animal life began to grow. Much of Britain's land became covered in thick forest and animals suited to a forest habitat, such as pigs, deer and boar, began to flourish. It was also a period of technological advancement as hunting weapons and tools became more complex and settlers began to build basic stone houses.

New Stone Age
4000–2500 BC

We know more about the New Stone Age – also known as the Neolithic Age – thanks to the huge number of artefacts that have survived from this period. This was the most technologically advanced period of the Stone Age – many new tools were created and decorative pieces such as pottery and stone statues were made. People began to farm the land by planting crops and raising livestock. Many types of settlement began to appear, including villages, houses and stone circles known as henges.

EVERYDAY LIFE

ARTEFACTS, HUMAN REMAINS AND RUINS GIVE US AN IDEA OF WHAT EVERYDAY LIFE WAS LIKE IN THE STONE AGE. This includes how and where people lived, what they ate, how they spent their time and the technology that they used to help them.

The inside room of a Stone Age house in Skara Brae, Orkney Islands

Food and Cooking

In the Old and Middle Stone Ages, people were hunter-gatherers. They survived by hunting, scavenging, fishing and gathering wild foods such as nuts, berries, eggs and fruit. The New Stone Age marks the introduction of new farming methods, which led to the growing of crops and the raising of livestock. Food, especially meat and fish, would have been cooked over a fire. Later on in the New Stone Age, the fire would have been lit and kept inside a **hearth** inside the home.

SHELTER AND HOUSES

During the Old Stone Age, hunter-gatherers led mostly **nomadic** lives and would have travelled the land hunting animals and collecting wild foods. They would have found shelter in caves to protect themselves from the cold, otherwise building temporary shelters out of tree branches, leaves and animal **hides**. In the New Stone Age, people began to settle in small villages and the first houses were built. These houses had stone walls, timber roofs and often consisted of only one room, which would have been used for eating, sleeping and socialising.

The First Farmers

From around 4000 BC, people stopped living as nomadic hunter-gatherers and began to settle in villages where they could farm the land around them. People learnt how to sow, harvest and store different types of crop, as well as breed and raise livestock, such as cows, pigs and sheep. The men would often tend to the crops and livestock, while the women would have ground grain to make flour or prepared and cooked the animals that had been killed. For the first time, people had easy and constant access to food sources, which meant that more people survived and the population grew rapidly.

CAVE ART

Stone Age people were not only skilled hunters and **craftspeople**, but skilled artists too. They painted on many cave walls around Europe, most likely in the caves that they found shelter in. They mostly painted the animals that they hunted, such as sabre-toothed cats and types of deer.

Paint was made from particular minerals that had been mixed with water or animal fat. There were only a few colours available to Stone Age artists as they could only use natural materials to make paint – they used soot to make black and chalk to make white. Other colours included browns, reds and yellows, which they made from earth and rocks. Art historians believe that they would have made paintbrushes out of twigs with feathers or even hair attached to the end.

This is a cave painting in Lascaux, France, a location known for its many cave paintings. Caves here are world-famous for housing some of the most skilled cave paintings from the Stone Age in Europe.

TOOLS AND WEAPONS

NEARLY ALL OF THE TOOLS AND WEAPONS IN THE STONE AGE WERE HAND CARVED AND CRAFTED FROM STONE, BONE OR FLINT.

FLINT

Many of the Stone Age tools and weapons found in Britain are made from a hard rock called flint. Flint was reasonably easy to sculpt into sharp-edged objects including axes, arrowheads and knives. Stone Age people would have struck and chipped the flint until it was the correct shape; a method which is known as knapping. Flint was found in many places across Britain and flint mines sprang up in areas where large amounts of flint had been found. Flint miners would dig for flint using **picks** made out of deer antlers and other animal bones.

Grime's Graves

Grime's Graves in Norfolk, England, is home to one of the largest Stone Age flint mines – around 433 **shafts** and 400 pits have been discovered at the site, the largest measuring in at over 14 metres deep and 12 metres wide. Miners would have dug for flint in a network of tunnels, which were held up by wooden platforms, and the deepest depths would have been reached using wooden ladders.

HUNTING TOOLS AND WEAPONS

Stone Age hunters and warriors developed inventive methods for making tools, such as spears, bows and arrows. Bows and arrows allowed hunters to seriously injure or kill animals, such as birds and deer, from a safe distance and with less risk of being injured themselves. Bows were made out of flexible wood with animal intestines attached as string, which would have allowed the hunters to fire arrows. The arrowheads were shaped into sharp points that would pierce the flesh of an animal. Stone Age hunters often relied upon their weapons to capture and kill animals.

This excavated pit at Grime's Graves shows the tunnel network at the flint mine. The tunnels would have led to many other pits deep underground.

Everyday Tools

Hand axes were common and extremely useful tools during the Stone Age. They were usually oval in shape and made out of flint. They would have been used for a variety of tasks, such as cutting through meat, chopping wood, hammering bone and digging holes. Stone Age hand axes of many different shapes and sizes have been found all over Britain, which shows that hand axes were an essential, multi-purpose and everyday tool for Stone Age people in Britain.

Other tools archaeologists have uncovered include many sharp, flint blades that would have been used like knives to cut food and other materials. They have also identified tools called scrapers, which look similar to flint blades but would have been used to remove hair and fat from animal hides so that they could be used for shelter and clothing.

A flint hand axe found in Winchester, England

FARMING INVENTIONS

It was only in the New Stone Age that more modern farming methods began to be used, which sparked the use of tools that helped Stone Age people to farm land more efficiently, such as the sickle. The sickle was a hand-held flint tool with a slightly curved blade on one side to help to cut the stems of crops more easily. This allowed farmers to harvest a larger number of crops in much less time than before.

This is an example of how a flint sickle may have looked. This sickle was found in the Middle East and would have been similar to those used in Britain during the Stone Age.

SKARA BRAE

THE VILLAGE OF SKARA BRAE IS A 5,000-YEAR-OLD PREHISTORIC SETTLEMENT FOUND ON THE ORKNEY ISLANDS, NEAR SCOTLAND.

The settlement was discovered in 1850 after a huge storm uncovered the ruins of the ancient village. Archaeologists have continued to excavate the village over the last 150 years and have uncovered eight houses, many tools, hundreds of pieces of pottery and many magnificent pieces of jewellery.

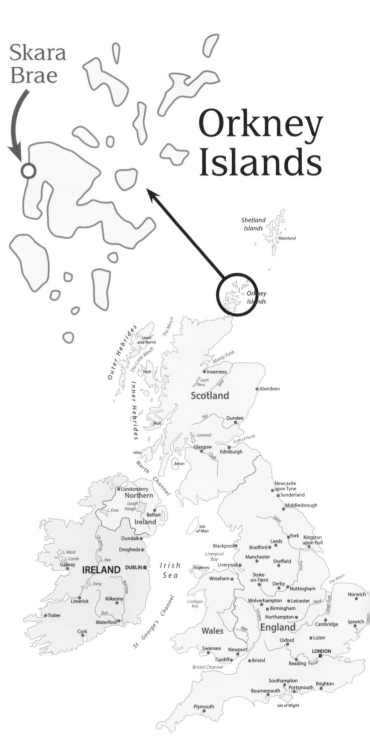

The prehistoric settlement of Skara Brae, Orkney Islands

Historians believe that people first settled in the village of Skara Brae during the New Stone Age — between 3200 BC and 2500 BC. As many as 10,000 people are estimated to have lived in the village over the course of 700 years. Historians have learnt about how they lived, what they ate and their religious beliefs from the many artefacts and ruins that still remain there today.

HOMES

The people of Skara Brae built houses with walls made out of large stones that they held together with a building material called midden. Midden was made from rotten rubbish, animal bones and broken bits of shell collected from the seashore. The houses had two circular stone walls; an inner one and an outer one. Midden was put in the gap between the two walls to strengthen the houses against extreme weather conditions and to prevent them from losing heat.

All of the eight houses that have been excavated in Skara Brae are connected to each other by long and often covered passageways.

Each house had one room with a hearth at its centre. The fire inside the hearth would have been used to keep the house warm and to cook on. Stone furniture, such as dressers, have been found along with stone boxes that would have been used for storage. Archaeologists have also found stone bed frames that would have been filled with dried plants to make them more comfortable to sleep on.

The ruins of the inside of a house in Skara Brae

EVERYDAY LIFE

Historians study the items that have been found on the Orkney Islands to help us to better understand what everyday life would have been like on the island. Everyday objects, such as tools and furniture, would have been made from natural materials found on the island.

The tunnels that have been found stretching between the houses at Skara Brae suggest that the people who lived there had a strong sense of community and spent a lot of time socialising with the people who lived around them.
Such a tightly-knit community was unusual in these early farming societies. Lots of other evidence from this time points towards individual farmsteads being preferred instead, but Skara Brae seems to have been a community where everyone worked and lived together.

These are examples of some of the tools that have been found at Skara Brae.

Food, Fishing and Farming

The villagers in Skara Brae would have spent their time working as farmers by raising cattle and sheep and growing crops like barley. They also fished along the island's coastline for shellfish like cockles, mussels, crabs and oysters as well as fish such as cod and saithe. Seabirds would have provided a rich source of protein for the villagers, who would have used the birds for both their eggs and their meat. We know so much about what the islanders ate because the bones of animals, as well as fragments of seabird's eggshells, have been found in the midden that was used as cement in the houses. The villagers had a more luxurious and rich diet than most Stone Age people because they had a greater amount of resources to use – they could farm the land, fish the seas and hunt the skies.

Grooved Ware Pottery

The people of Skara Brae made a type of Stone Age pottery known as grooved ware pottery. It was usually flat-bottomed with straight sides that sloped outwards and featured an intricate, grooved decoration around the top or the sides. These pots may have been used as **vessels** for serving or drinking water, as food bowls or as a part of **rituals**, which seems likely as many have been found at burial sites.

CLOTHES AND JEWELLERY

No items of clothing have ever been found at Skara Brae, probably because the materials that would have been used to make clothes in the Stone Age would have rotted away. Villagers may have worn clothes made out of animal furs and skins, which would have protected them from the cold and stormy weather on the island. Bone pins have been discovered all over the island and probably would have been used to pin together pieces of clothing.

Archaeologists have also excavated beads and pendants from the site. Most of the items found were carefully carved from bone to make elaborate pieces of jewellery. Many of the beads that have been found are made from bones and teeth, which would have had holes drilled into them so that they could have been strung together on a necklace.

> A Stone Age necklace

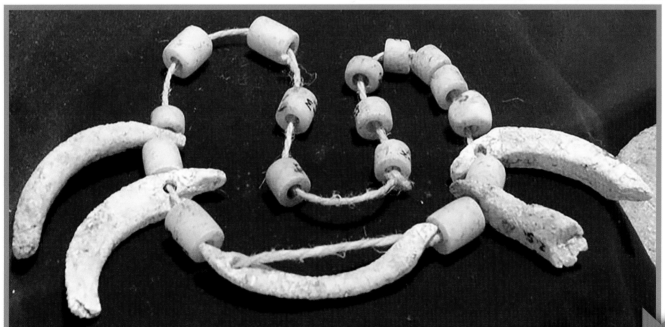

THERE IS STILL MUCH THAT WE DON'T KNOW ABOUT STONE AGE PEOPLE'S RELIGIOUS BELIEFS AND PRACTICES. However, we do have some knowledge of their burial practices thanks to the tombs and monuments that have been discovered by archaeologists.

LONG BARROW TOMBS

Neolithic people **cremated** their dead and buried their ashes in specially built long barrow tombs, which were usually rectangular in shape and covered with a mound of earth. Each barrow tomb had a number of wooden or stone chambers inside where up to 50 members – probably of the same family or village – were buried over a long period of time.

Once a person or a group of people were placed inside a chamber, its entrance would have been covered by a large stone **cairn**. The mound would have been built using earth that had been dug out from around the chamber and placed on top of the tomb, which would have left a ditch running around the outside of the barrow tomb.

A long barrow tomb in Dorset, England

Barrow tombs were constructed by barrow builders and were seen as a type of monument, as the cairns and large earth mounds could be seen for kilometres around. Richer families would have often been buried with objects, called grave goods, including pottery, bows, arrows, tools and jewellery, which they thought they may need in the **afterlife**. The great care early Neolithic people took to bury and honour their dead tells us that religion is likely to have played a large part in their everyday lives.

A Neolithic cinerary urn, which would have been used to hold the ashes of the dead after they had been cremated

Stone Circles and Henges

Prehistoric people began to build henges at the end of the New Stone Age. Henges were ditches that surrounded a circular area that was usually filled with large, upright slabs of stone called megaliths. Many historians believe that these circles held great significance for people during the Stone Age and were used in religious ceremonies and rituals. Ceremonies may have taken place for religious reasons and could have been headed by a priest or used to mark the changing of the seasons.

MEGALITH MYSTERIES

In 2015, around 90 stone boulders, each roughly 4.5 metres long, were found buried near Stonehenge, the famous Bronze Age henge site in Wiltshire, England. The boulders had been deliberately toppled and buried at the site, but both historians and archaeologists are puzzled by how they were transported to the site and their significance for prehistoric people. Historians have named this site 'Super-Henge' and have dated it to the late Neolithic period.

An impressive stone henge found in Skåne, Sweden

A megalithic stone henge on the Isle of Lewis and Harris, Outer Hebrides, Scotland, that dates to around 3000 BC

THE BRONZE AGE

THE BRONZE AGE BEGAN AROUND 3000 <u>BC</u> AND IT MARKS A PERIOD OF HISTORY WHEN PEOPLE BEGAN TO MAKE OBJECTS OUT OF METAL.

The first metal that people used was copper and most of the artefacts that have survived to this day are made from it. During the Middle to Late Bronze Ages, people discovered that copper could be mixed with another metal, tin, to make bronze, which could be used to craft stronger and more hard-wearing items.

The Great Orme copper mines in northern Wales were opened up during the Bronze Age to keep up with an increasing demand for bronze goods in Britain and across Europe.

HOW WERE BRONZE OBJECTS MADE?

Copper and tin, the metals that are used to make bronze, had to be extracted from different types of rock, known as ores. Prehistoric metalworkers would crush the copper or tin ore until the metals were released. The metals would then have been heated over a fire at an extremely high temperature until they melted, a process called smelting. The liquid metal would have been poured into moulds or shaped individually by hand into bronze tools, weapons, vessels, display objects or ornate pieces of jewellery.

A Bronze Age sword, known as a rapier, that was found in Cambridgeshire, England

LIFE IN THE BRONZE AGE

Life in the Bronze Age was much more advanced than in the Stone Age, mostly because of the technological progress made possible by metalworking techniques, improvements in agriculture and the growth of trade. Bronze Age people would travel across Britain and Europe to trade important **commodities**, such as gold and amber, in return for bronze and bronze work.

This amber and jet necklace, dated to around 1500 BC, was discovered in Cambridgeshire, England.

At the start of the Bronze Age, most people lived with their families. This changed, however, as people started to live with other families in village communities. It was also the first time that there had been a social difference between people; some were rich and some were poor. Most rich communities got their wealth from trading bronze and copper items within Britain and Europe.

A Late Bronze Age golden oath ring dated to around 950–700 BC

BEAKER CULTURE

THE BEAKER PEOPLE LIVED DURING THE BRONZE AGE. They have been named after the highly distinctive, bell-shaped pots they made.

THE BEAKER PEOPLE

They first appeared in western Europe around 2800 BC and were one of the earliest known groups of people to use metal to make tools and other objects. Much of what we know about the Beaker culture comes from human remains and artefacts, such as Beaker pots, tools and weapons, that have been found in the graves of Beaker people at burial sites across much of Britain and Europe.

A replica Beaker pot showing the distinctive style of pottery that the Beaker people were known to produce

The Amesbury Archer

The Amesbury Archer was an Early Bronze Age man whose skeleton was excavated from a burial site near Stonehenge. He is believed to have lived around 4,300 years ago and originally came from an area near to the **Alps**, perhaps travelling long distances to England to trade goods. He was buried with around 100 objects including Beaker pots, flint arrowheads, copper knives and gold hair ornaments. Because of the number and value of the objects he was buried with, historians think he was probably a rich **trader**.

The skeleton of the Amesbury Archer and some of the goods that were buried with him, including the distinctively shaped Beaker pots

THE AMESBURY ARCHER HAS BEEN NICKNAMED THE 'KING OF STONEHENGE', AS HISTORIANS BELIEVE HE WAS A RICH AND POWERFUL MAN DURING THE EARLY BRONZE AGE.

TRADE AND TRAVEL

The Beaker people were thought to be the first real explorers and travellers in the prehistoric period. Beaker culture is believed to have been brought to Britain from other parts of western Europe around 2500 BC. Beaker people are believed to be one of the first groups to learn how to smelt metals such as copper, bronze and gold, as well as produce pottery. They would have traded their metalwork and pottery, which would have then been transported across the seas in wooden log boats and traded for other goods.

The remains of a 3,000 year old Bronze Age wooden log boat, which would have been used by the Beaker people to transport their goods by sea

Beaker Pots

Beaker pots are one of the objects that Beaker culture is most associated with. They are distinctive in style, with a bell-like shape, and are patterned with grooved lines. They would have been made out of clay before being placed in a fire in order to harden them into pottery. They would have been used to hold drinks, such as mead and beer, food and other objects.

Bell-shaped, patterned Beaker pot

TECHNOLOGY AND TRANSPORT

THE BRONZE AGE WAS A TIME OF SIGNIFICANT TECHNOLOGICAL ADVANCEMENT AND GREAT INNOVATION.

TRANSPORT AND TRAVEL

In 2016, the oldest wheel ever found in Britain was uncovered at a Bronze Age archaeological site in East Anglia and it was dated to around 1100–800 BC. The wheel was one metre in diameter and had been unusually preserved in its complete form by the **silt** in the ground. Archaeologists believe that the wheel was once part of the earliest known vehicle, the horse-drawn cart, as horse bones have also been found close by. Horse-drawn carts would have allowed for the faster transportation of food, weapons and building materials.

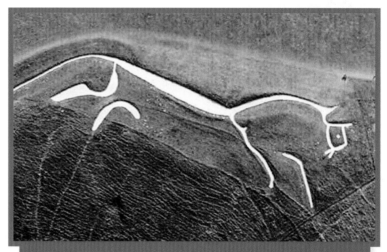

The Uffington White Horse, seen above, can be found on a hillside in Oxfordshire and dates back to the prehistoric period. It is made from deep trenches filled to the top with crushed white chalk. Historians are not quite sure why it is there, or even whether it actually is a horse, but some believe it represents the importance of horses and transport within Bronze Age society.

Over 15 Bronze Age boats have been discovered in Britain, many of which are Ferriby boats. These boats would have been built from oak planks that were sewn together with tough yew branches and fixed with wooden wedges. The new seafaring technology would have allowed Beaker people to travel to Britain and begin to settle. It would have also opened up new routes, by which they could trade bronze and copper.

Tools and Weapons

In the Early Bronze Age, the discovery of metal, particularly of copper, tin and then bronze, allowed people to create a much greater range of strong and hard-wearing tools and weapons. Miners collected different types of metal and metalworkers used it to make and craft objects. Many objects that were made could be used for more than one purpose and everyday tools often became useful weapons in battle.

Axes would have been used as an everyday tool to chop down trees and cut logs into smaller pieces of wood, which would then have been used for building materials or as firewood. However, axes would have also been used as fearsome weapons in times of war. Metalworkers hammered the edges of axe heads and created thin sockets in the handle in order to securely attach the axe head to the shaft.

This Bronze Age axe head was found in Wisbech, England, and the marks made by the hammer that was used to shape it can still be seen.

Bronze daggers were particularly popular during the Bronze Age and would have been used as light-weight, sharp-edged weapons that could cut through small objects or stab people during wartime. They were also important as a means of showing off a person's wealth and status and would often have been polished in order to give the appearance of a golden surface.

A typical example of a Bronze Age dagger found in Cambridgeshire, England

SOCIETY AND SETTLEMENTS

EVERYDAY LIFE IMPROVED GREATLY FROM THE STONE AGE TO THE BRONZE AGE. People who lived during the Bronze Age had more food, a greater range of tools and weapons and had improved houses in which to live.

VILLAGE PEOPLE

Bronze Age families settled in villages and usually lived amongst a number of other families in larger communities. These communities were often made up of several families and usually had a village leader. Most people would have spent their time farming, raising livestock and growing and harvesting crops, such as wheat and barley.

However, villages may have also had a number of skilled tradespeople who could have been metalworkers, miners, weavers or potters. Villagers' social lives would have been centred around the home, with families and communities cooking and eating together, sharing stories and perhaps even playing games.

Homes

Families in the Late Bronze Age would have lived in round huts with cone-shaped roofs, known as roundhouses. The walls were built using wood plastered with mud and they had a thatched roof made out of straw, reeds or grass. Together, the combination of mud plaster and the thatched roof would have made the houses waterproof and warm. There would have been one room inside each house with a hearth in the middle that could have been used for cooking, warmth and light.

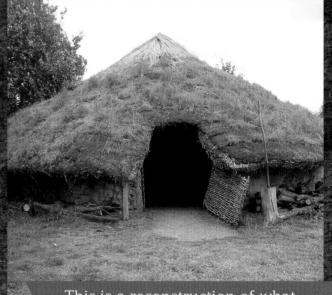

This is a reconstruction of what a typical Bronze Age roundhouse would have looked like at Flag Fen, East Anglia, England.

FLAG FEN

In 2006, archaeologists began to excavate a site in East Anglia, England. Since then, they have uncovered one of the largest and best-preserved Bronze Age settlements ever found in Britain. It has been named Flag Fen and the land is believed to have been first settled on around 3,500 years ago.

Much of what we know about Bronze Age settlements and everyday life has been revealed or confirmed by the many discoveries made at Flag Fen. So far, archaeologists have uncovered glass beaded pots, parts of roundhouses, many bronze weapons as well as tools and the stored remains of grain, bones and even human faeces (poo). All of this reveals important information about what everyday life was like for the settlers of Flag Fen.

Rising sea levels meant that the land around Flag Fen eventually became flooded marshland by the Middle Bronze Age. In 1300 BC, raised paths, called causeways, were built from planks of wood so that the people could still walk around Flag Fen. The causeways at Flag Fen were made out of around 60,000 wooden planks. The dead were also buried in the marshes by the causeways with grave goods such as weapons, tools and pottery.

SO MANY ARTEFACTS AND OTHER PIECES OF EVIDENCE HAVE BEEN FOUND AT FLAG FEN BECAUSE THE CLAY QUARRY THAT THEY WERE BURIED IN HAS KEPT THEM VERY WELL-PRESERVED.

STONEHENGE

STONE HENGES CONTINUED TO BE BUILT DURING THE BRONZE AGE AS WELL AS THE STONE AGE. The most famous prehistoric henge in Britain is called Stonehenge and it is located in Wiltshire, England.

Stonehenge is around 5,000 years old and was built in several stages over hundreds of years throughout the late Neolithic and Early Bronze Ages. Historians are still not sure exactly why Stonehenge was built, but many believe Stonehenge was used for many different things including religious ceremonies, as a burial ground or for rituals to mark the changing of the seasons.

Stoneheng

STONEHENGE WASN'T BUILT IN A DAY ...

Over hundreds of years, the many builders of Stonehenge used two types of stone to construct the henge; smaller stones known as bluestones and larger stones made out of sandstone known as sarsens. Stonehenge consists of two circles that were built at different times; an inner circle built from sarsens and an outer circle built from bluestones. In around 2150 BC, 82 bluestones were transported hundreds of kilometres from the Preseli mountains in south-west Wales to build the inner circle. Around 2000 BC, the sarsen stones were added to the monument and were transported from the closer Marlborough Downs in north Wiltshire, England, over 32 kilometres away. To this day, how the extremely heavy bluestones (and the sarsen stones) were transported over such huge distances remains a mystery.

Sarsen stones stand upright at Stonehenge and are each around 9 metres tall.

DEAD AND BURIED

Many archaeologists and historians believe that Stonehenge may have functioned as a burial ground. This is because around 65 cremated human remains have been found at the site and as many as 150 people are believed to have been originally buried there, making it the largest prehistoric cemetery in Britain. Some people believe the stones commemorate the deaths of important members of the same family, community or religious order because of the size of the monument and the effort taken to build it.

Summer and Winter Solstices

Some people also believe that religious ceremonies took place every year at Stonehenge to mark the summer and winter solstices, in June and December. Solstices occur twice every year when the Sun reaches its highest or lowest point in the sky, these are also the longest and shortest days of the year. Some historians believe that the position the stones have been placed in is linked to the position of the Sun during both the summer and winter solstices. Solstice celebrations still take place at Stonehenge for this reason.

People still gather at Stonehenge to celebrate the solstice.

PREHISTORIC BRITAIN:
A TIMELINE

837,000 BC

The first sign of human life appeared in Britain in Happisburgh, Norfolk.

16,000 BC

Some of the earliest cave paintings appear in the Lascaux Caves, France.

6000 BC

Britain became separated from mainland Europe by water.

3650 BC

Around the time Long Barrows are believed to have been built.

3200 – 2500 BC

People first began to settle in the village of Skara Brae, Orkney Islands.

OLD STONE AGE

MIDDLE STONE AGE

NEW STONE AGE

500,000 BC

The Boxgrove Man is thought to have lived.

12,000 BC

The first people began to settle in Britain.

4000 BC

Introduction of farming and new farming tools.

3500 BC

Prehistoric people began to build stone or wooden henges.

2800 – 2500 BC

Historians believe this was the time period in which 'Super-Henge' was built.

2500 BC

The building of Stonehenge first began.

2300 BC

The Amesbury Archer is thought to have lived.

2000 BC

Sarsen stones were transported to Stonehenge to complete the final stages of construction.

1100 – 800 BC

The oldest wheel ever found in Britain is dated to this period of time.

(It would have looked similar to this one).

1000 – 800 BC

The Uffington White Horse, Oxfordshire, England was built using white chalk.

EARLY BRONZE AGE

MIDDLE BRONZE AGE

LATE BRONZE AGE

2500 BC

Beaker people began to travel to and settle in Britain.

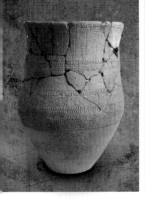

2150 BC

82 bluestones were transported from Wales to Stonehenge.

1500 BC

People began to settle on the large Bronze Age settlement of Flag Fen, England.

1000 BC

The oldest seafaring wooden log boat sailed the seas, later found in Dover, England.

43 **AD**

The Roman invasion of Britain and the introduction of the written word mark the end of the prehistoric period.

FIND OUT MORE

WEBSITES

Learn more about the mysteries of Stonehenge on these websites:

www.english-heritage.org.uk / visit / places / stonehenge / history-and-stories / history /
www.stonehenge.co.uk / about-stonehenge

Visit this BBC website to find out more information about prehistory:

www.bbc.co.uk / history / ancient / british_prehistory

Places to Visit

Find out more about visiting the places you have learnt about in this book by looking at the following websites:

Flag Fen
www.flagfen.org.uk

Grime's Graves
www.english-heritage.org.uk / visit / places / grimes-graves-prehistoric-flint-mine

Skara Brae
www.historicenvironment.scot / visit-a-place / places / skara-brae

Stonehenge
www.english-heritage.org.uk / visit / places / stonehenge / plan-your-visit

GLOSSARY

AD	means after Christ was born
afterlife	a religious belief that there is life after death
Alps	a large mountain range that lies across Europe
archaeologists	people who study human history from the discovery of objects from the past
artefacts	objects made by humans, typically ones of cultural or historical interest
BC	means 'before Christ' was born
cairn	a mound of rough stones usually built as a memorial or landmark
cave-dwellings	caves that prehistoric people would have used for shelter
commodities	materials or products that can be bought and sold, such as bronze
craftspeople	people who are skilled at making things by hand
cremated	to have burnt a dead body to ashes
estuary	the mouth of a large river
excavating	uncovering something by digging away and removing the earth that covers it
flint	a hard rock used to make tools during the Stone Age
hearth	the floor of a fireplace
hides	animal skins
historians	people who study history
hunter-gatherers	humans who get their food by hunting wild animals or gathering plants
nomadic	to live the life of a person who has no permanent home, but moves from place to place
picks	pointed tools
prehistoric	any period of history that occurred before the appearance of writing
primitive	basic or early in development
rituals	a series of ordered actions that take place during religious ceremonies
ruins	the remains of structures or buildings
scavenged	to have fed on animals that were already dead
shafts	upright tunnels
silt	fine sand or clay
trader	a person who trades
vessels	containers used for food or drink

INDEX